Animal GIANTS

By William Caper

MODERN CURRICULUM PRESS

Pearson Learning Group

The following people from Pearson Learning Group have contributed to the development of this product:

Art and Design: Stephen Barth, Dorothea Fox, Alison O'Brien

Editorial: Leslie Feierstone Barna, Nicole Iorio, Jennie Rakos

Inventory: Levon Carter

Marketing: Alison Bruno

Production: Roxanne Knoll

All photography © Pearson Education, Inc. (PEI) unless otherwise specifically noted.

Photographs: Cover: © age fotostock/SuperStock, 6: © Peter Arnold, Inc., 8–9: © Peter Arnold, Inc., 10: © D. Allen Photography/Animals Animals, 12–13: © William Ervin/Photo Researchers, Inc., 14: © Nigel J. Dennis/Photo Researchers, Inc., 17: © Reuters/Corbis, 18–19: © M. Watson/Ardea, 20: © Rexford Lord/Photo Researchers, Inc., 22: © Peter Arnold, Inc. Illustration: 4: Jennifer Fairman.

ISBN-13: 978-1-4284-0927-9

ISBN-10: 1-4284-0927-0

Printed in the United States of America
1 2 3 4 5 6 7 8 9 10   11 10 09 08 07

Pearson Learning Group

1-800-321-3106
www.pearsonlearning.com

Contents

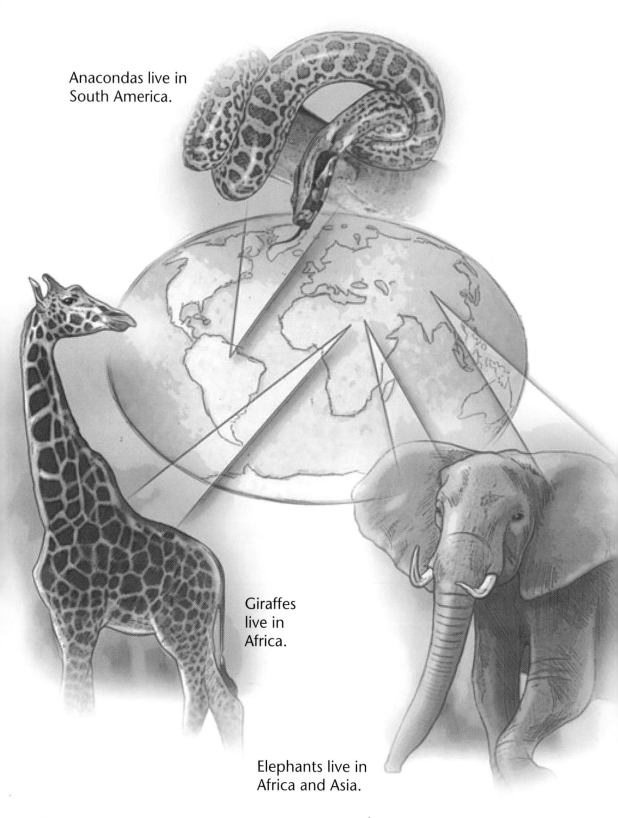

Anacondas live in
South America.

Giraffes
live in
Africa.

Elephants live in
Africa and Asia.

Giant Animals

Being a giant animal means many things. For some giant animals, it might mean doing things in special ways. For others, it might mean having **adaptations** that help the animals **survive**. An adaptation is any change that helps an animal have a better chance to survive. For example, an animal might use one part of its body to do different things.

There are **advantages** to being a giant animal. Giant animals can often do things that other animals cannot do. Giant animals are often better than other animals at getting food or facing **predators**. Predators are animals that kill and eat other animals.

There are also **disadvantages** to being a giant animal. Life is not always easy for these animals. Giant animals can have problems because of how much they weigh or how tall they are.

Elephants, giraffes, and anacondas are three animal giants. Each animal is different in its own way. Each does special things to survive.

Elephants

The elephant is the largest animal that lives on land. The only animal that is taller is the giraffe. However, giraffes weigh much less than elephants. Elephants can weigh up to 12 tons.

Elephant Adaptations

Elephants have special adaptations because of their great size. These adaptations help them survive. They use their trunks, ears, legs, and feet in special ways. Each one of these body parts has many uses.

Elephants use their trunks to drink water.

Elephants can breathe, smell, eat, drink, and cool off with their trunks. Elephants have a very good sense of smell. Sometimes they wave their trunks in the air to sniff for food or predators. They can smell people who are more than a mile away.

Elephants pick up food with their trunks and put the food into their mouths. They also sip water into their trunks. They then bend their trunks and put the water into their mouths. Elephants can even use their trunks to cool off. They hold their trunks high in the air and spray themselves with water.

Elephants have giant ears. Their giant ears help them hear very well. They can hear sounds that people cannot hear.

Two other elephant adaptations are in their legs and feet. Their legs are round, solid, and strong. Each foot has a thick pad of tissue. These thick pads of tissue help hold the elephants' weight. The tissue is also the reason an elephant makes very little noise when it walks.

Elephants' feet **expand** when they are standing. The elephants' weight makes them swell, or become larger. Yet, the foot will **contract** as elephants lift their leg. This helps elephants pull their feet out when they are stuck in mud.

Elephants easily scare
away most predators.

Advantages of Being Big

One of the most important advantages for elephants is that they have very few predators. There are not many animals that will attack an elephant. Elephants' size and strength keep most other animals away.

Elephants can use their strength to lift heavy things. Using their tusks, elephants can lift as much as one ton. One ton is the same weight as a small car! Elephants also use their trunk to carry things. Some Asian elephants help people this way. They easily carry logs that weigh hundreds of pounds.

Elephants' strength can also help them find food. They sometimes use their heads to push down small trees. Then they eat the leaves at the top of the tree. Elephants eat lots of plants. This makes open space in their habitat. Other animals can then move their homes to the new open space. In this way, elephants' strength even helps other animals that share their habitat.

Elephants can use their large ears to cool off.

Disadvantages of Being Big

There are some disadvantages to being big. Elephants need a lot of food and water to survive. Elephants must sometimes travel very far for food. They can eat about 300 pounds of plants a day. They can also drink as much water as would fill a large fish tank.

Elephants can also have problems moving around easily because of their size. They cannot fully turn their huge heads. They can see only to the front and to the sides.

Defenses

Elephants use their great size as a **defense** to scare off predators. Groups of elephants form a circle around the baby elephants to protect them from a **threat**. Their huge bodies make a wall that keeps the baby elephants safe. Elephants can stick their ears out to look even bigger than they are. Many predators also fear being kicked or stepped on by the elephants' giant legs.

Living Large

To "shake hands" elephants wrap their trunks together.

Giraffes

While elephants are the largest land animals, giraffes are the tallest land animals. Giraffes' necks are about 6 feet long. That's taller than most people!

Giraffe Adaptations

Giraffes also have adaptations that help them survive, such as their long tongues. Their tongues can be as long as 21 inches. That is almost as long as two rulers end to end. Giraffes use their long tongues to pull the leaves off tall trees and other plants.

Giraffes also have big hearts. A giraffe heart is 2 feet long. Their hearts work hard to pump blood up those long necks to reach their head. Their hearts beat up to 170 times per minute. That is twice as fast as a human heart.

◀ A giraffe's neck helps it get to food that other animals cannot reach.

Giraffes take turns watching for predators when they drink.

Advantages of Being Big

Giraffes' long necks let them reach leaves that other animals cannot reach. Giraffes are so big that they have few predators. Lions are one of a giraffe's few predators.

Disadvantages of Being Big

Giraffes' size is also a disadvantage. They have to spread their front legs far apart to drink. In this position, it is difficult for giraffes to move suddenly if predators appear. Giraffes also need to eat a lot to survive. Sometimes they must walk for miles to find enough food.

Defenses

Giraffes' main defenses are their spots and their legs. The spots let the giraffes hide among trees. The color pattern of the spots helps the giraffes blend in with trees so they are hard to see when they are standing still. Giraffes' long legs help them run from predators. They can run at about 30 miles per hour.

Living Large

Giraffes can move 15 feet with a single step.

Anacondas

The biggest snake in the world is an anaconda. Anacondas can be about 29 feet long. They can weigh up to 550 pounds.

Anaconda Adaptations

Anacondas have many adaptations that help them survive. They have a special way to catch their **prey**. They also have special adaptations that help them eat their food.

Anacondas are a type of constrictor snake. Constrictors usually do not bite prey to kill it. Constrictors wrap themselves tightly around the prey. Then they swallow the prey whole.

Anacondas do not chew their food. Instead, they swallow the animal slowly. Sometimes it takes more than half an hour for an anaconda to swallow an animal. Anacondas can breathe while they swallow prey. They have a tube in the bottom of their mouths. This tube takes in air.

Anacondas and all snakes have a special adaptation that lets them swallow animals that are larger than their heads. Their top and bottom jaws are joined by tissue. This tissue expands and lets anacondas open their mouths very wide.

Like their jaws, anacondas' ribs are easily spread. After anacondas swallow a big meal, their ribs spread out. This lets their bodies make room for the prey.

Anacondas can survive for a long time without food. Reptiles, unlike mammals, are cold blooded. A reptile's body temperature changes as the temperature of the air changes. Cold blooded animals do not use much energy to keep their body temperature the same, so they don't need as much food as other animals, like mammals. Snakes also store fat in their bodies. When snakes do not eat, they can live off this fat. These adaptations work to help the anacondas survive.

Anacondas can grow to be more than 12 inches around!

Advantages of Being Big

Being a big anaconda has its advantages. Grown anacondas do not have many predators. Many animals are afraid of anacondas because of the anaconda's giant size. Anacondas can also eat large prey, such as big mammals.

Disadvantages of Being Big

There are also disadvantages to being big. Many people are afraid of the huge anaconda. People often hunt anacondas simply because they are afraid of them.

These heavy reptiles cannot move fast on land. So anacondas like to stay in water. However, anacondas must wait for their food to come to them. Anacondas need to lie very still and surprise their prey when it comes into the water.

◀ Anacondas often live in swamps or slow moving rivers.

Anacondas will lie very still
to wait for their prey.

Defenses

Anacondas use their size and strength for
defense. If attacked they hold the animal still with
their mouth. They then wrap their strong body
around the predator so it cannot breathe.

Living Large

This huge snake can even be a threat
to elephants! In one Asian language,
anaconda means "elephant killer."

Being Big

There are many advantages to being a giant animal. It often means having few predators. The animal's great size can act to scare away attackers. Giant animals can also use their size to defend themselves. Elephants make a wall of their large bodies to protect their babies. Giraffes can run away fast. Anacondas wrap their big bodies around their attackers.

Being a giant animal can also be a big disadvantage because giant animals often cannot move as easily as smaller animals. Elephants cannot jump or fully turn their heads. It is not easy for giraffes to drink water. Anacondas have a hard time moving quickly on land.

Having adaptations makes it possible for giant animals to survive. Giraffes have big hearts. Elephants' feet contract and expand. Anacondas' jaws and ribs expand to help them swallow their prey. These animals have all found the best ways to survive as giant animals.

Habitat loss means we could lose many animals.

Giant Animal Habitats

Being a giant animal also means needing a large habitat. Elephants, giraffes, and anacondas need a lot of space to live and grow so they can survive. These animals are losing their habitats.

The main cause of habitat loss is people. Humans often move into parts of animal habitats. People build homes and offices there. Today, habitat loss is a threat to many animals, including elephants, giraffes, and anacondas.

People are not animal giants. We are not even among the largest animals on Earth. However, we can protect animal giants—and all the animals—that share our world.

Living Large

One in five humans lives in or near the habitat of the Asian elephant.

Glossary

adaptations changes that help an animal live

advantages things that make something easier to do

contract to make smaller

defense a way to protect from an attack

disadvantages things that make something harder to do

expand to make bigger

predators animals that kill and eat other animals

prey an animal that is hunted and eaten by other animals

survive to stay alive

threat a danger